DISASTERS

FIRE
DISASTERS

ANN WEIL

SADDLEBACK
EDUCATIONAL PUBLISHING

DISASTERS

SADDLEBACK
EDUCATIONAL PUBLISHING
www.sdlback.com

ISBN-13: 978-1-61651-931-5
ISBN-10: 1-61651-931-2
eBook: 978-1-61247-627-8

Printed in Guangzhou, China
0712/CA21201056

16 15 14 13 12   1 2 3 4 5

Photo Credits: page 38, Bettmann/Corbis; page 66, © David Jones
| Dreamstime.com; page 77, © Willeyj | Dreamstime.com; page 87,
© Tupungato | Dreamstime.com

CONTENTS

CHAPTER 1 | Introduction

DATAFILE

Timeline

December 19, 1974

A movie called *The Towering Inferno* is released about a fire in an office building.

July 20, 2000

Mesa Verde National Park in Colorado closes after a wildfire grows from 50 acres to 500 acres in three hours.

Where is Colorado?

HERE

Key Terms

fine—to demand that someone pays money for breaking a law

inferno—intense heat

wildfire—a fire that spreads very fast, making it difficult to put out

CHAPTER 1 | Introduction

People have relied on fire for many thousands of years. Early humans used fire to warm themselves and cook their food. They also used fire to frighten away animals that might hurt them.

Fire is a basic part of modern life. People still use fire to cook and to heat their homes.

Fire can also be a killer. A house fire can turn deadly if people do not get out in time. Fires seriously burn many people. These injuries are very painful and take a long time to heal.

Every year fires destroy many homes and businesses. Fire is expensive. Fires cause more damage than floods, tornadoes, and other disasters combined.

Wildfires

Toasting marshmallows and telling scary stories around a campfire is a lot of fun. But campfires can burn out of control. Wildfires destroy forests and parks. Wildfires also kill many animals.

Some wildfires are caused by lightning. Careless people are also responsible for many wildfires. Dropping a lit cigarette outside on a hot, dry day can start a huge wildfire.

Sometimes people start wildfires on purpose. They may think it's fun. But these fires are no joke. Many homes are destroyed by wildfires. Firefighters risk their lives battling wildfires. People caught starting wildfires are fined or sent to prison.

Fires and Earthquakes

Earthquakes caused some of the worst fire disasters in history. Big cities are most at risk for fires after an earthquake.

Earthquakes damage gas lines. Gas leaks lead to explosions and fires. Earthquakes also damage water pipes. After an earthquake there may not be any water to use to fight the fires. San Francisco, California, and Tokyo, Japan, are two big cities that suffered huge fires after earthquakes.

Office Buildings on Fire

A popular disaster movie of the 1970s was called *The Towering Inferno*. It was about a fire in a high-rise office building.

Office buildings have safety features to protect people from fire. Sprinklers are designed to turn on automatically. Water sprays over a fire to put it out. There are usually fire escapes and fire stairs so people can exit a burning building quickly.

When terrorists crashed two planes into the World Trade Center, the jet fuel exploded and set the twin towers on fire. This real-life towering inferno was the worst fire disaster ever.

The first full-time fire brigades were started back in the 1800s. Firefighters today are well trained and highly skilled. They use modern equipment to control fires that threaten lives and destroy property.

Wildfire, Summer 2000

The summer of 2000 was one of the worst for wildfires. Hot, dry weather in the westerns states was mostly to blame. By the end of the summer, 74,180 fires had burned more 6.5 million acres across the United States.

CHAPTER 2 | London Bridge Fire, 1212

DATAFILE

Timeline

July 1212

Both ends of the London Bridge catch on fire,
making it impossible to escape.

September 2, 1666

The Great Fire of London begins in a bakery.

Where is London?

HERE

Did You Know?

During the Great Fire, people tried to stop the flames by destroying their houses. This way, the fire would not have anything to burn.

Key Terms

fire break—a strip of land cleared to stop a fire

plague—a disease that spreads quickly and causes death

thatch roof—a house covering made of straw

CHAPTER 2 | London Bridge Fire, 1212

Many European cities grew up around rivers. Boats moved up and down these rivers long before there were cars or trains.

The Thames River runs through London, England. London is a very old city. Many of London's beautiful buildings and bridges are hundreds of years old.

London Bridge was built in the 1170s. This bridge was more than just a way to cross the Thames River. It became a kind of neighborhood.

Hundreds of families lived in houses built on the bridge. There were many shops on the bridge, too. Thousands of people used the London Bridge every day. It was a very busy place.

London Bridge is on Fire!

One windy day in July 1212, London Bridge caught fire. Both ends of the bridge were burning. People on the bridge were trapped. The wind blew the fire toward the center of the bridge.

Buildings on the bridge caught fire. The bridge's narrow street filled with smoke and flames. People panicked. Some jumped off the bridge.

About 3,000 people died from the London Bridge fire. Many were burned or crushed to death. Some drowned in the Thames River below.

All the houses on the bridge were destroyed. But parts of the bridge survived the fire. The huge stone piers were left. People could still use the bridge. It remained an important crossing for another 600 years.

Fighting Fires Without Water

There were no water hoses back in the Middle Ages when the London Bridge fire occurred. People used buckets of water to put out fires. But this did not work for very big fires.

Houses were made of wood with thatch roofs. Wood and dry straw burn quickly and easily. Once a fire started, it was difficult to control. Entire streets could go up in flames.

People tried to stop fires from spreading. People worked together to pull down houses. They used large hooks attached to long poles and chains. This made a fire break. They hoped the fire would not be able to cross the big gap they created. If they were lucky, the fire would burn itself out.

Unfortunately, this did not work in 1212. The London Bridge fire spread through the city. Most of London burned to the ground.

London introduced new fire laws after the 1212 disaster. People built roofs using stone tiles instead of straw. Every neighborhood had to keep its own hooks for pulling down buildings in an emergency.

The Great Fire of London, 1666

The Great Fire of London was not nearly so deadly as the London Bridge fire. Fewer than ten people died in the 1666 blaze.

The fire started in a bakery. The baker did not put out the fire in the oven before he went to bed. His shop caught fire. The flames spread.

It became a huge fire that burned through London. Thousands of homes were destroyed. Churches and other buildings were ruined. The Great Fire burned down entire neighborhoods.

There were many rats. Rats carried germs that made people sick.

The year before the Great Fire, a terrible plague had killed thousands. The Great Fire of London killed a lot of the rats causing the plague.

After the fire, people rebuilt houses. The streets of London were cleaner than before. There were far fewer rats and less disease after the Great Fire of London.

Ocean liner passes under the Tower Bridge.

DATAFILE

Timeline

May 7, 1933

President Roosevelt explains the "New Deal," a plan which will give jobs to more than 3 million Americans.

September 8, 1934

A mysterious fire starts in the library on the *Morro Castle* cruise ship on its way back to New York.

Where is New York?

Did You Know?

Lawmakers created stricter cruise ship safety rules following the *Morro Castle* fire.

Key Terms

fireproof—made so that it does not burn

Great Depression—a period in the 1930s when many people did not have jobs

luxury—giving a feeling of comfort

smuggling—the practice of carrying something illegal into or out of a country

CHAPTER 3 | The *Morro Castle*, 1934

The *Morro Castle* was a luxury cruise ship. It was built in 1930. It sailed between New York and Havana, Cuba.

Hundreds of people enjoyed a floating vacation aboard the *Morro Castle*. They ate the finest food. They danced to music played by a live band. But the last voyage of the ship was a horror.

The history of the *Morro Castle* reads like a mystery story. And the mystery of the *Morro Castle* has never been solved.

The Great Depression

It cost a lot to travel to Cuba and back on the *Morro Castle*. Most people did not have enough money to go on the *Morro Castle*.

The 1930s were a difficult time for many Americans. It was the Great Depression. The stock market crashed. People lost their savings. Many people were out of work.

Those lucky to have jobs had to settle for very little money. Most Americans were struggling. But some rich people still had money to spend. And sailing on the *Morro Castle* was one way for them to escape the Great Depression for a few days and have fun.

However, the crew was not having fun. They were paid very little money to work on the ship. The crew was given bad food while the others feasted.

Some of the *Morro Castle* crew tried to make extra money by smuggling. They got things in Cuba and hid them on the ship to bring back to the United States to sell.

The crew even smuggled people into America on board the *Morro Castle*. They could make a lot of money this way. But it was against the law. If they were caught, they would go to jail.

The captain of the *Morro Castle* tried to keep order on ship. It was a difficult job. And the crew hated the captain for doing it.

The Captain is Dead!

Friday, September 7, 1934, was the last night of the cruise. The *Morro Castle* was due back in New York at eight o'clock the next morning.

It was time for dinner. But the captain was not at his table. One of the crew went to look for him. He found the captain dead.

Was the captain murdered? No one knew for sure. He may have had a heart attack. There were rumors that he was poisoned. But even today his death is a mystery.

Fire!

The chief officer took over the *Morro Castle*. His name was William Warms. Warms was second in command. Now that the captain was dead, it was his job to get the ship safely back to New York. Unfortunately, he was not good at his job.

A fire started in the ship's library. No one knows for sure how the fire began. It might have been an accident. Someone might have dropped a lit cigarette. Or the fire might have been set on purpose. The cause of the fire is one more part of this unsolved mystery.

One of the crew told Warms about the fire. Warms was not worried about the fire. The *Morro Castle* was supposed to be fireproof! Warms didn't even try to put out the fire. This was a big mistake.

There was a storm that night. Chief Officer Warms was more worried about the storm than the fire. He was not used to sailing the ship. He was in a hurry to get back to New York. The *Morro Castle* sailed for New York at top speed.

The winds from the storm fanned the fire in the library. More and more books caught fire. The flames spread. Soon the whole ship was on fire. The fire was out of control. Now there was no way to put it out.

The firefighting equipment did not work. There was no water running to the fire hoses up on deck. Were they just broken? Or had someone turned them off on purpose? This was another mystery, like the death of the captain.

By this time it was around three o'clock in the morning. Most of the passengers were sleeping. No one sounded an alarm.

The crew took the lifeboats for themselves instead of doing their jobs and waking the sleeping passengers. Six lifeboats carried 85 people safely away from the burning ship. Only 5 of the 85 were passengers. The rest were crew, including officers.

The *Morro Castle* was only a few miles from shore. But it never made it back to New York. One hundred thirty-four of the 549 people on board died.

The End of the *Morro Castle*

The *Morro Castle* sank just off the coast of New Jersey, close to a hotel. People could see the burning ship from the shore.

A large crowd gathered on the beach. Some people started selling ice cream and hot dogs to people as they watched the end of this disaster.

Word of the disaster spread. More and more people came to see for themselves. By that afternoon, a quarter of a million people had turned up. The army was called in to move the crowd away.

The burned out shell of the ship became a tourist attraction. People bought tickets to see the place where all those people died.

It's Still a Mystery

William Warms and some of the other officers were sentenced to jail. They should have done more to save the passengers. They were partly to blame for the disaster. But the mystery of the captain's death was never solved.

CHAPTER 4 | Chicago, 1871

DATAFILE

Timeline

1869

The Chicago Water Tower is built. It becomes one of the only buildings to survive the fire.

October 8, 1871

The Great Fire of Chicago begins in a barn.

Where is Chicago?

Did You Know?

The Great Fire of Chicago started in the O'Leary barn. Even though the fire destroyed much of the city, the O'Leary house was not burned.

Key Terms

historian—an expert in history

lantern—a light inside of a glass or paper case

mill—a building where grain is ground into flour or meal

CHAPTER 4 | Chicago, 1871

The Great Fire of Chicago started as a small barn fire. It began around 9:00 p.m. on Sunday, October 8, 1871.

By midnight, much of the city was on fire. Firefighters worked all night to control the fire. Rain started to fall two days later. This helped put out the last of the flames.

When it was all over, 300 people were dead. Ninety thousand were left homeless. More than three square miles of the city were in ruins. The fire destroyed property worth almost $200 million.

Mrs. O'Leary's Cow

A popular song blames the Chicago fire on a woman milking her cow.

"One dark night, when people were in bed,
Mrs. O'Leary lit a lantern in her shed,
The cow kicked it over, winked its eye, and said,
'There'll be a hot time in the old town tonight.'"

Historians doubt that this was really how the fire started. But they do agree that it started in Mrs. O'Leary's barn.

How did an ordinary barn fire turn into the Great Fire of Chicago? From the beginning, everything went wrong.

Firefighters were already very tired from fighting another big fire the previous night. That fire had started in a mill Saturday evening.

The firefighters were up all Saturday night and through Sunday afternoon. Many of them had not eaten or slept when they heard that the O'Learys' barn was on fire.

The fire engines and equipment were not ready to fight another big fire so soon either. One of the fire engines broke down. Some of the fire hoses were not working well.

Another problem was that the fire was not reported right away. Then the firefighters went to the wrong place. By the time the firefighters arrived at the barn, the fire was already out of control.

If the firefighters had gotten to the fire earlier, they could have put it out quickly.

The barn was full of hay and coal. Both burned and made the fire very big and very hot. The wind spread the fire.

Was the Cow to Blame?

Mrs. O'Leary said she did not cause the fire. She and her husband said they were asleep in bed when the fire started. They were probably telling the truth.

If Mrs. O'Leary had been in the barn when the fire started, she could have put it out. At least she would have run to get help right away. She would have wanted to save her barn, her animals, and her milk business.

So then how did this story get started? A Chicago newspaper reported that a cow had kicked over a lamp. Straw on the floor of the barn caught fire, then the barn itself, and eventually the city.

Peg-Leg Daniel Sullivan

A key suspect was Daniel Sullivan. Daniel Sullivan had a drinking problem. He lived near the O'Learys. He may have started the fire when he was smoking in the barn.

Daniel refused to take the blame for the fire. He told this incredible story instead. He said he was across the road when he saw the flames. He ran into the barn to save a calf.

His wooden leg got stuck in a crack in the floor. He had to take it off to escape. He hopped out clinging to the neck of a rescued calf.

The City Rebuilds

Chicago was rebuilt after the fire. Like London after their Great Fire, the new city of Chicago was safer and more beautiful. Today little evidence of the disastrous fire remains. But people do still occasionally sing the song.

The city of Chicago in ruins after the Great Fire of 1871.

The Chicago skyline today.

DATAFILE

Timeline

November 18, 1903

The United States and Panama sign a treaty to build the Panama Canal.

December 30, 1903

Iroquois Theater in Chicago goes up in flames during a play.

Where is Panama?

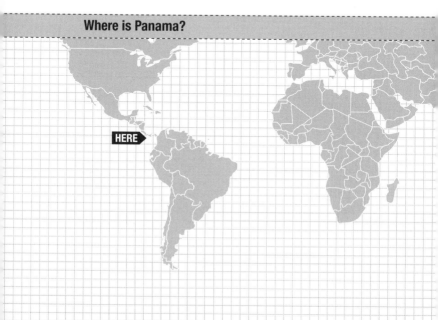

Key Terms

canvas—a heavy cloth used for painting

intermission—a break between two acts of a play

scenery—painted backdrop used on the stage of a play

CHAPTER 5 | Iroquois Theater, 1903

Some disasters seem more tragic than others. The 1903 Iroquois Theater fire was especially sad. Many of the victims were children and their mothers.

It was December 30th. Schools were closed for the holidays. That afternoon's show was sold out.

More than 1,900 people crowded into the six-story theater. They were there to see a musical comedy. There would be singing and dancing. They were looking forward to a fun time.

Instead, it turned into a horrible nightmare.

Theater Fires

There had been many tragic theater fires before. Theater fires were a big problem in the United States and Europe.

Most fires started high above the stage. Theaters have lots of lights near the ceiling. These lights shine on the actors on stage. They are very bright. And they can get very hot.

There was also a lot of painted scenery above the stage. During the show, the old scenery was pulled up. New scenery came down. Sometimes the scenery accidentally touched these hot lights. The paint on the canvas burned easily.

By 1903, theaters kept firefighters near the stage, just in case. New theaters also had to have a fireproof curtain.

If a fire broke out, the curtain would come down quickly. This kept the fire from spreading into the audience.

The Iroquois was a new theater. It had just opened about a month before. It should have had the newest fire safety equipment. But it didn't. And what was there didn't work properly.

In 1903, the Iroquois Theater was a disaster waiting to happen.

Fire! Fire!

It was about 3:15 in the afternoon. A fire started just after intermission. Everyone was back in their seats for the second half of the show. Some of the actors were on stage. The band was playing.

The fire started small. A piece of canvas brushed against a light high above the stage. A worker up there saw the tiny flame. He tried to crush it with his hand. But it was just out of reach.

The fire spread quickly. A light crashed down to the stage. The star of the show looked up and saw the fire. He told people not to panic. He urged them to stay in their seats. The band continued to play.

There was a fireman on duty. But he didn't have good equipment. He had only a small amount of powder for sprinkling on flames to put them out.

The powder didn't work. There were no fire hoses. There was no way to put out the fire.

The curtain never reached the floor. It got stuck on its way down. Some survivors said it caught fire. Maybe the workers lowered the wrong curtain.

Some of the burning scenery fell onto the singers and dancers. They rushed from the stage. There were about 500 people working behind the scenes. Almost all of them got out alive. They ran out a door behind the stage. But the tightrope walker stuck high above the stage died.

The blast of cold air from that open door blew the fire into the audience. Flames and smoke whipped through the seating area and up into the balcony.

Children cried out for their mothers. Mothers screamed for their children. The audience panicked. The lights had gone out. No one could see in the smoky darkness.

There were iron gates over many of the exit doors. Some of these gates were locked. Others were hard to open.

Many of the doors opened inward. People were already pressed against the doors. There was no way to open these doors either. The only way out was through the main doors.

About two-thirds of the audience managed to escape. They were the lucky ones.

In only 15 minutes, 600 people were dead. Many were trapped behind doors that would not open. Some of them were still in their seats.

Life Goes On

The fire department arrived. They quickly put out the fire. The theater was not badly damaged. It reopened less than a year later. But it changed its name to the Colonial Theater. It was torn down in 1925 to make room for a new theater.

DATAFILE

Timeline

September 15, 2000

The summer Olympics begin in Sydney, Australia.

December 25, 2001

Bushfires rage near Sydney.

Where is Sydney?

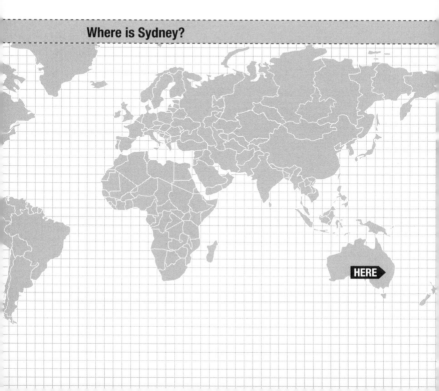

HERE

Key Terms

bush—wild land in the countryside

equator—an imaginary line around the middle of the earth. It is equal distance from the North and South Pole

rage—to be out of control

CHAPTER 6 | Australia Bushfires, 2001

Sydney, Australia, was home to the 2000 Olympics. The Games were a great success. Millions of people around the world saw this beautiful city on television.

In 2001 this same city faced disaster. Fires broke out in the "bush," or countryside, near the city. These fires, called bushfires, were closing in on Sydney. Smoke filled the sky and blocked the sun. Many people were forced to leave their homes. It was too dangerous for them to stay.

Summer Christmas

The fires started on Christmas Day. Australia is south of the equator. When it's winter in America, it's summer in Australia. Australian summers are hot and dry. Australia has many bushfires in

November, December, and January. But not all of these turn into disasters.

Thousands of firefighters spent Christmas Day battling the blazes instead of celebrating with their families. Strong winds made it very difficult to control the fires. Firefighters from other parts of Australia came to help. About 22,000 firefighters were on the ground and in the air fighting the fire. Water was dropped from airplanes and helicopters.

The fires raged for two weeks. More than 1.2 million acres of bushland burned. About 170 properties were lost.

This was not the first time Christmas fires had threatened Sydney. More than 800 fires started between December 27, 1993 and January 16, 1994.

December 1997 brought even worse fires to the city. Fires raged in bushland on three sides of Sydney.

But the 2001 Sydney bush fires may not have been an accident. Police suspected that arsonists might have started many of them. Arsonists set fires on purpose. A special arson squad, Strike Force Tronto, worked to find the arsonists.

Police arrested more than 20 suspects. Most were between nine and 16 years old. A new plan required children guilty of arson to meet hospital patients with severe burns. This way, they would see the result of their crimes. Adults were sentenced to up to 14 years in prison.

Volunteer Firefighters

Australia has thousands of volunteer firefighters. These brave men and women risk their lives for no pay. They have other regular jobs they do most days. Some work in stores or banks. Some are teachers. They risk their lives fighting fires because they care about helping other people. Many of them feel that this is the most important thing they do. Thanks to their efforts, Australia has lost very few lives to bushfires.

Australian firefighters travel to other countries, including the United States, to teach others what they do. Not only do they save lives in their own country, their experience and know-how helps save lives all over the world.

DATAFILE

Timeline

February 17, 2003

A stampede erupts in a Chicago nightclub.

February 20, 2003

Fire breaks out at The Station nightclub in Rhode Island.

Where is Rhode Island?

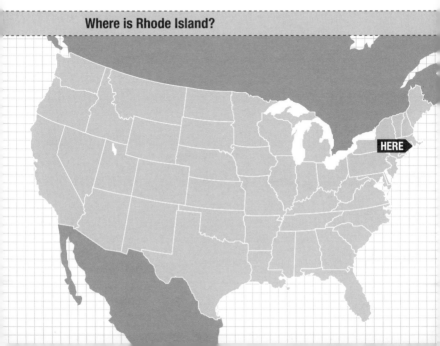

HERE

?

Did You Know?

The Station was a small wooden building. It was not required to have a sprinkler system because it was built before 1976.

Key Terms

foam—a soft, sponge-like material

heavy metal—a kind music that is very loud with shouted singing

CHAPTER 7 | Warwick, 2003

About 100 people died when a fire broke out at a club in Rhode Island. It was one of the worst club fires in recent history. A heavy metal band was playing at The Station nightclub. They set off sparklers at the start of their show. Sparks flew everywhere. Some of them hit soft foam on the walls. This started a fire. Thick, poisonous smoke from the burning foam filled the club.

The club was on fire! People panicked. They raced for exits. Every second counts during a club fire. Too many people and too few exits is a deadly combination. The band's speakers blocked one of the emergency exits near the stage. Most of the people tried to get out the front doors.

Some of the dead burned to death. Others died from breathing the fire's poisonous smoke. Some may have been crushed to death in the rush to escape the burning building. One of the dead was a member of the band that was playing that night. Some of the dead bodies were so badly burned they could not be identified.

About 180 survivors were very badly burned, too. Some of them had no skin left on their faces.

This disaster made people more aware of the danger of club fires. Fire inspectors closed several clubs since The Station fire. Those clubs were not safe. One of them might have been the next club fire disaster.

The Cocoanut Grove Fire: Boston, 1942

This deadly fire started small, too. Someone at the nightclub took a light bulb out of its socket. He wanted his corner of the room darker. A young waiter went to put a light bulb back in. He lit a match to see where it went. The flame touched one of the fake palm trees. It caught fire. The fire spread to other fake palm trees. Silk curtains turned into sheets of flames.

The club was full of people. They panicked. Everyone rushed to the exits. But emergency doors had been bolted shut. Others were hidden behind curtains. People didn't know they were there.

The only way out was a very slow revolving door. When firefighters arrived, they broke down the revolving door. They found a heap of dead bodies piled six-deep behind it.

There were 900 people in the club that night. About half of them died in the fire.

The Cinq-Sept Club Fire: France, 1970

Sometimes it takes a disaster to get people to make changes. After the Boston Cocoanut Grove club fire, American clubs became safer. There were more fire exits. Unfortunately, other countries did not learn from the Cocoanut Grove tragedy.

On November 1, 1970, a popular band was playing at a nightclub in France. Two hundred fans packed the club. The club did not want people sneaking in without paying. So they locked all the emergency doors. There was only one way in and out of the club.

Someone dropped a lit match. It landed on a cushion. The cushion caught fire. Flames shot up the plastic sheets. In less than a minute, the hall was on fire. Black smoke filled the club.

The smoke from the burning plastic was poisonous. People could not see or breathe. About 150 people died instantly. Some ran to the exit. But the turnstile jammed. Only 60 people escaped.

DATAFILE

Timeline

1769

Europeans establish settlements in what is to become San Diego County.

1942

After the bombing of Pearl Harbor, San Diego is chosen as the mainland headquarters of the Pacific Fleet. It's now home to the largest US Navy base.

Where is San Diego County?

HERE

Key Terms

arson—criminal act of setting a fire on purpose

low humidity—dry air, air with little water content

Santa Ana wind—warm to hot, dry winds that blow from east to west in Southern California

CHAPTER 8 | California Burning

California has a long history of wildfires. California's dry brush and forest are vulnerable to hot, dry summers. The famous Santa Ana winds blow in from the desert. This dries things out even more. Wildfires have even figured in books and songs about California.

California 2003 Fire Siege

In late October 2003, a series of wildfires broke out in Southern California. The largest of these fires was the Cedar fire. It started in the hills east of San Diego on October 25.

These fires spread quickly. Thick smoke in the air made it difficult for firefighters to see. Helicopter pilots were grounded by poor visibility.

These were "ground fires." Ground fires are the most destructive of wildfires. They can burn brush down to the rock underneath.

Strong Santa Ana winds blew the fires at over 50 miles per hour. Hundreds of homes were burning. Thick ash and smoke made roadways hard to see. The ash looked like dirty snow. Air traffic was disrupted across the United States as smoke and ash spread.

Power lines were knocked over. Phone communications were down. Hundreds of thousands of Southern Californians started evacuating. Some tried to drive off in their cars. Tragically, they were trapped by the flames. More than 10 people died in their burnt-out cars.

A California Department of Forestry tanker drops fire retardant on a hillside brush fire.

Thousands of residents evacuated to a parking lot at Qualcomm Stadium, a local professional football stadium. The National Guard brought in food, water, and clothing. Other residents ignored police orders and stayed at their homes. They sprayed water from garden hoses to keep the flames away. Despite their best efforts, eventually many of these homeowners were also forced to leave.

After seven days, officials reported 24 people dead, including one firefighter. The fires charred land from Santa Barbara to San Diego. It was Southern California's deadliest wildfire ever.

Over 3,700 homes were destroyed in the 2003 Fire Siege. More than 700,000 acres of land were burned. Famous national parks including the Cleveland National Forest burned out of control. In the San Bernardino National Forest alone, 90,000 acres went up in flames. Damage caused by the fires was estimated to be over $2 billion.

Fire officials said the fires were most likely caused by lightning strikes. Lightning strikes are common during Southern California summers. But arson was also to blame. A man was arrested. He said he was hunting and his gun accidentally went off. He was lying. The man was sent to jail.

The Wildfires of 2007

Four years later, major wildfires again struck Southern California. Incredibly, it happened on nearly the same day as the 2003 wildfires.

On October 22, more than a dozen wildfires whipped through Southern California. This included the hard-hit area of Witch Creek. The combination of high winds, low humidity, and high temperatures caused the wildfires to spread quickly.

Thousands of firefighters were having trouble getting the blazes under control. Winds up to 70 miles per hour blew hot embers onto the dry brush. In seconds, the brush ignited. Fires in San Diego County burned 300 homes to the ground within hours. There were no deaths yet. But thousands were homeless.

Hundreds of thousands of acres were now on fire. Planes and helicopters dropped water and fire retardant on trees and dry brush. But the fires kept spreading. Some emergency vehicles were trapped on the highways.

Along the coastline, burning ash rained down on the famous Pacific Coast Highway. The police had to close it. In a nearby shopping center, fires jumped onto trees and torched them. Cars in the parking lot were also burned.

Major power lines throughout Southern California were damaged. Many people lost electricity to their homes and businesses.

From the air, fires could be seen for more than 150 miles. In the beach town of Malibu, gusting sea winds caused the fires to change direction. The winds were heading directly toward Pepperdine University. At the last second, the fires changed direction again. The university was safe.

As in the 2003 fires, many residents evacuated to Qualcomm Stadium. Food, clothing, and medicines were handed out. Others went to the US Marine base at Camp Pendleton for help. Approximately 50 shelters took in more than 20,000 displaced residents.

In the Witch Creek Fires over 3,000 homes and other buildings were destroyed. Total evacuations were the largest in California history. Hundreds of thousands of residents were evacuated.

In all the fires, over 500,000 acres of land were burned. Seventeen people were confirmed dead. And more than 140 firefighters were injured.

Police said the fires were caused by downed power lines and arson. Five people were arrested for setting fires. However, none of the major fires were set by arsonists.

CHAPTER 9 | Drought-Baked Texas

DATAFILE

Timeline

April 14, 1935

One of the worst dust storms in American history inflicts ruin on Kansas, Texas, and Olkahoma.

March 2008

A powerful winter storm develops in Texas that ultimately hits most of southern and eastern North America with heavy snow, rain, hail, and tornadoes.

Where is Texas?

HERE

Did You Know?

The word Texas comes from the Native American Caddo word *tejas,* meaning friends or allies. Today, the Caddo Nation resides in Oklahoma.

Key Terms

livestock—farm animals

panhandle—a narrow strip of land from one state or territory projecting into another

vegetation—plants and plant life

CHAPTER 9 | Drought-Baked Texas

Texas is America's second-largest state after Alaska. Because of its size and geography, Texas experiences extreme weather. Texas gets everything from snow to hurricanes. Tornado Alley passes right through northern Texas. Texas averages nearly 140 tornadoes each year. Texas also endures severe droughts. It also suffers many wildfires. But the 2011 wildfires were the worst in the state's history.

In 2011, a devastating drought baked Texas. Texas was suffering its worst drought since the 1950s. The drought left brittle, dry brush all over Texas. This vegetation started to decay, making it easier for a spark to ignite it.

In April 2011, in east Texas, near the Louisiana border, wildfires burned thousands of acres in the forested area of Piney Woods. Almost all of the 1,500-acre Possum Kingdom State Park burned. Walls of flames climbed 40 feet high into trees and buildings.

In west Texas, flames overtook ranches and farmland, killing livestock. Thousands of acres were also burning in the northern panhandle and in the southern area around Houston. Satellite photographs showed white clouds of smoke rising from every part of Texas.

The Texas wildfires were especially dangerous. Shifting winds moved walls of fire in all directions. Firefighters would start out fighting a fire right in front of them. In minutes, the flames would move to the side or behind them. Some firefighters reported that the wildfires moved like a living thing.

In one area, flames roared toward a group of firefighters. The fires were too hot and too close. Walls of flame surrounded them. They were ordered to retreat. Several firetrucks were trying to get away. But they couldn't see each other or the road. One firefighter was hit by a truck and killed. The rest of the firefighters escaped safely.

Another firefighter died a week after the fire-truck he was in got stuck. He tried to run away. But he was burned very badly.

Tens of thousands of residents were evacuated. Families only had time to take some clothes, their pets, and a few other possessions before escaping. Some residents were driven away by rescue vehicles. Other survivors drove their cars through thick, dark smoke to escape. The cars were very hot inside. Pets and children were at risk for heat stroke. Luckily, police on roadways guided most drivers to safe locations.

Many evacuees drove to high schools and churches for shelter. The Red Cross set up trailers to assist evacuees. They cooked thousands of meals for survivors. Water and clothing were handed out. Some evacuees argued with fire officials. They wanted to go back to their neighborhoods to check on their homes. Many went back and found their homes had burned to the ground. Charred fireplaces were often the only thing left standing.

The Bastrop fire left a trail of devastation.

By the end of the summer, 3.5 million acres had burned. Parts of the state had experienced 100 straight days of temperatures over 100 degrees Fahrenheit. Cattle were dying. Farmers had no water to grow hay and grass to feed them.

Then, in early September 2011, a series of wildfires started burning through west and central Texas. The largest of these fires burned in the town of Bastrop. Bastrop is only 30 miles from the state capital of Austin.

The first day, firefighters were unable to contain the raging wildfires. The flames were too hot. Firefighters could not get close enough to fight the blazes. The wildfires spread from isolated regions to more populated ones. Some burning areas were over 16 miles wide.

Nearly 1,700 homes in Bastrop burned. More than 5,000 people were evacuated. Over 35,000 acres were on fire. In Bastrop State Park, walls of fire shot up 10 feet in the air. Half of Bastrop State Park's 6,000 acres were incinerated. Two people died in the Bastrop fire.

High winds from Tropical Storm Lee pushed the wildfires' flames across Texas. Besides Bastrop, more than 50 other Texas wildfires were burning.

The wildfires were moving so fast they even jumped Texas's Colorado River.

Firefighters from every state fought the blazes. Airplanes and helicopters dropped water and bright orange fire retardant onto the flames. But helicopter pilots had several problems. Thick, gray smoke made it hard to see. Pilots were also finding it hard to get water. Many of the surrounding lakes had dried up. Helicopters were flying long distances to find water. This caused delays in fighting the wildfires.

Gradually, the winds died down. Temperatures got cooler. Firefighters were able to get the fires under control. More than 30,000 acres in Bastrop County burned in just over a week. Texas fire officials said brave, hard-working firefighters prevented 30,000 other Texas homes from burning down.

Ten people died in the 2011 Texas wildfires. Four firefighters died. More than 2,000 homes were destroyed.

DATAFILE

Timeline

July 1851

The colony of Victoria is established. Days later, the discovery of gold triggers a huge rush of people.

February 2009

High temperatures and winds over 60 miles per hour fanned the flames of multiple bushfires that ultimately burned over one million acres.

Where is Victoria, Australia?

Key Terms

containment—keeping something harmful under control

extinguish—to cause something to stop burning

premier—a prime minister or other head of government

CHAPTER 10 | Black Saturday, Victoria, Australia

The state of Victoria in Australia has a diverse landscape. Thickly forested hills mix with sandy deserts and rocky cliffs near the Tasman Sea and Indian Ocean. Victoria covers more than 250,000 square miles in the southeastern corner of Australia.

A Deadly Heat Wave

Wildfires are not unusual in Australia. Thousands of bushfires burn there every year. Some cause damage. Others are extinguished quickly, with no serious problems.

But during late January and early February 2009, a historic heat wave was baking southeastern Australia. In the southern hemisphere it was the middle of summer. Temperatures in January were regularly over 110 degrees Fahrenheit. Health authorities reported hundreds of deaths from the heat wave.

In the first week of February, the premier of Victoria announced a fire emergency. Weeks of no rain and record high temperatures had set up the possibility of deadly bushfires. The premier called bushfire conditions "the worst in the history of Victoria."

The Fires Ignite

On February 7, thousands of firefighters spread out over the southeastern Australian bush, or countryside. Hundreds of heavy-duty fire trucks arrived. Airplanes and helicopters flew over Victoria ready to drop water and flame retardant.

Temperatures kept rising. At one point, it was 115 degrees in the city of Melbourne. Winds blew at over 60 miles per hour. Trees and power lines twisted dangerously in the wind.

At mid-day, firefighters called in with an emergency update. A series of power lines had been knocked over. A spark had set off a blaze in the brush. And it was spreading quickly. The flames rushed toward northeast Melbourne, which quickly started to burn.

Residents called emergency phone lines with descriptions of a "horrible orange glow" heading right for them. Planes and helicopters dropped tons of water and fire-retardant foam on trees and brush. But the fires kept burning.

Natural tree oils like eucalyptus acted like fuel for the fires. Trees were actually bursting into flames. The heat was so extreme that it killed people 1,000 feet away.

The Kilmore East fire burned the towns of Kinglake and Marysville northeast of Melbourne to the ground. Dozens of people died, and hundreds of homes were destroyed. In Kinglake alone, more than 800,000 acres of land burned. In Marysville, 45 of the town's 500 residents were killed.

All over Victoria, gray plumes of smoke mixed with cloud cover. There was practically zero visibility. Rescuers and residents had a hard time finding each other. Planes and helicopters were grounded because the pilots could not see out the windows.

In a few hours, hundreds of homes and thousands of acres of land were nothing but gray ash. Thick smoke covered many roads. Residents tried to escape by car. Many ended up driving into the raging orange flames. Dozens of burnt-out car shells littered Victoria's roadways.

Firefighters kept battling the bushfires. They used all their skills, including "drip-torching." This is when hand torches are used to purposely start small fires. The small fires eat up brush that is normally consumed by a larger fire.

Other firefighters built containment zones around the fires. Containment zones are a kind of earthen wall or dam. They kept the fires inside the zones and easier to control.

As evening approached, the spreading bushfires started to slow down. Some of the cloud cover began to thin out. Helicopters lifted off and dropped water and retardant on the remaining flames. Other helicopters plucked stranded residents from their burning homes.

Temperatures started dropping. Winds were dying down. In Melbourne, the temperature dropped from over 110 degrees to around 85 degrees in less than half an hour. The bushfires were almost under control. And rains were predicted for the following week.

The town of Kinglake West is only 28 miles from Melbourne's central business district (seen here). Metropolitan Melbourne is home to more than four million people.

As the bushfires died down, Australia's fire authorities announced some grim statistics. More than 173 people had died. Over 2,000 homes were burned to the ground. At least 3,500 other buildings were destroyed. It is estimated that over one million acres of land in Victoria burned.

Overall, nearly 80 townships in Victoria were affected by the bushfires. Thousands of residents were forced to flee their homes. Saturday, February 7, 2009, would go down in history as Australia's "Black Saturday."

Was It Arson?

Police determined that one of the major causes of Victoria's deadly bushfires was arson. Arson is when a fire is set deliberately. It is a serious and potentially deadly crime. Eventually a suspect was caught and charged with murder.

Climate scientists in Australia predict that fire danger throughout the country will increase in the future. One reason is that global warming is making temperatures hotter. Another is that remote communities in the Victorian bush do not have good fire safety plans. The bush is also becoming a more popular place to live, which increases the chance of dangerous fires.

Glossary

arson—criminal act of setting a fire on purpose

bush—wild land in the countryside

canvas—a heavy cloth used for painting

containment—keeping something harmful under control

equator—an imaginary line around the middle of the earth. It is equal distance from the North and South Pole

extinguish—to cause something to stop burning

fine—to demand that someone pays money for breaking a law

fire break—a strip of land cleared to stop a fire

fireproof—made so that it does not burn

foam—a soft, sponge-like material

Great Depression—a period in the 1930s when many people did not have jobs

heavy metal—a kind music that is very loud with shouted singing

historian—an expert in history

inferno—intense heat

intermission—a break between two acts of a play

lantern—a light inside of a glass or paper case

livestock—farm animals

low humidity—dry air, air with little water content

luxury—giving a feeling of comfort

mill—a building where grain is ground into flour or meal

panhandle—a narrow strip of land from one state or territory projecting into another

plague—a disease that spreads quickly and causes death

premier—a prime minister or other head of government

rage—to be out of control

Santa Ana wind—warm to hot, dry winds that blow from east to west in Southern California

scenery—painted backdrop used on the stage of a play

smuggling—the practice of carrying something illegal into or out of a country

thatch roof—a house covering made of straw

vegetation—plants and plant life

wildfire—a fire that spreads very fast, making it difficult to put out

Index